# LOVESICK

# LOVESICK

## Poems by Howie Good

THE POETRY PRESS
2009

Hollywood, California

Published by

THE POETRY PRESS
of Press Americana

the press of

Americana:
The Institute for the Study of
American Popular Culture
7095-1240 Hollywood Boulevard
Hollywood, CA 90028

http://www.americanpopularculture.com



Cover photo of Antelope Canyon
Courtesy Ingo Meckmann

Library of Congress Cataloging-in-Publication Data

Good, Howie.
Lovesick : poems / by Howie Good.
p. cm.
ISBN 978-0-9789041-6-6
I. Title.
PS3607.O5628L68 2009
811'.6--dc22
2009024666

# TABLE OF CONTENTS

**Part 1
Apocalypse Mambo**

**Part 2**
**A Tiny Fugue for Tomorrowland**



**Part 3**
**Ghosts of Breath**

**Part 5**
**Sleep Rituals**

# Part 1

# APOCALYPSE MAMBO

**A NOTE TO READERS**
Don't look here for ideas,
there are no ideas here,

only dark slashes of rain,
and scavenger birds

able to speak
but often unwilling,

and my heart,
thirteen years old again

and in a dirty red hoodie,
glad for the rain

and the burning wind
that brings it.

# TWO LAMENTS AND A SONG
# (IN 30 WORDS EACH)

**I *Beware the Dog***
When I go to pet the dog, it flinches.
I, too, have suffered the darkness of hands

and repent the memory,
a porch light carelessly left on during the day.


**II *My Autumn***
The season of rain and death,
and I'm like that tree there, shaking,

arms raised abjectly in surrender,
its children kidnapped by the wind.


**III *Song***
Whereupon I enter her night,
and, most suddenly,

bells wake, blaze like neon,
and though heretofore

an addled angel, halo half-askew,

she thereafter shimmering
under me fierce wings outspread.

**SNAPDRAGON CLAWHAMMER**
I stagger out the door under an armload of poems,
feverish red ones, friendless gray ones,
dark purple ones like the aftertaste of a scream.

Women cross the street to avoid me.
Cars honk in derision. Nobody asks, Hey,
do you need help with those?

Even the panhandler outside the 7-Eleven
points and snickers, and a little girl
hides her frightened face in her mother's skirt.

Later, hurled bottles will explode at my feet,
there'll be police and questions, but for now,
the jocks in the high school parking lot

are still scheming, and I stare as if in challenge
into the hooded eyes of storefronts,
nod hello to words – snapdragon, clawhammer –

almost too beautiful and broken to repeat.

**THE NEWS AT 11**
The world is a rifle butt
smashed in your face

a panting hand reaching
for your only child

And now the weather

What if our hearts weren't
such paper-thin bags

of blood and vomit
what if they were shiny

like the water-bright coats
of prancing red horses

## DITTY

Let's disappear, Barbara,
in a giant whoosh of flame

and look back and laugh
at the scribble of our smoke trail.

For once, let's not answer
the questions at the end of the chapter,

or even phone in to work,
but just climb the twisted ladder

of bones and shadows,
and if we must get somewhere,

let's do it secretly
like your lost gold earring.

## LOVE DURING WARTIME

Time to crack open that bottle
the previous tenant bequeathed us.

We can drink to whatever you want –
lack of sleep, importune prayers,
another day of freedom from the landlord's

fretful knock – then tumble into bed,
our bones loosened, our minds in happy
disarray, despite, or perhaps because,

it's now light, and there's a kind of war
outside our window, and the invisible sniper
in the gaunt bell tower is always watching

with bloodshot eyes for a clean shot.

## FOR THE WOMAN WHO WALKED OUT DURING MY READING

To what should I attribute it,
an upsurge in sunspot activity

or the general decay of manners?
Please don't say it was me,

the dull sincerity of my words,
their untreated depression,

that sent you rushing off.
Let me think there was a man

(with a ponytail, perhaps),
a vase of dried wildflowers,

a bedroom wall on which
you put a hand for balance

as you stepped out of your skirt,
your micro panties, and then yourself

and delicately into a love poem.

**HAIRCUT**

There's no wait this early.
I hang up my coat and climb into the chair.

He flips a gold barber's drape over me
with a practiced twist of his wrists.

I've known him a long time, 22 years,
ever since we moved to town.

Talking to my reflection in the mirror,
he says they've found a spot on his pancreas.

He asks what the pancreas does.
I try to remember from 10th grade biology.

My wife, he starts to say, but stops
and shakes his head, and then the only sound

is the bonelike clicking of the dancing scissors.

**A CURE FOR BOREDOM**
Invite a word inside, doesn't matter which,
they all suffer the same strange inability

to distinguish between bright and dark,

but if it refuses to tell where the loot is hidden,
or even how many birds constitute a flock,

shove its fingers in a drawer and slam the drawer shut
so that neighbors can hear a concerto of pain,

and when you're done, and it's mashed and misshapen
like a nail repeatedly and inexpertly struck,

fix it a drink and might as well have one yourself.

## LOVESICK

It isn't love if our embassy isn't burning,
if the windows haven't exploded

in a shower of diamonds from the heat,
if the ballerina isn't staggering around on stage

as from an accidental elbow in the face,
or if the knife-thrower, subject to ironic applause,

doesn't suddenly doubt the accuracy of his aim;
it isn't love if the moon isn't breathing,

if we don't receive unsought help from machines,
an automated summons to appear in court

and our bewildered joy upon entering the night
a moment after everyone else has left.

**IDENTITY**
One day it just happens,
a man I never met before,
or wanted to meet,

mistakes me for someone else,
an old classmate's adopted brother,
and that night for the first time

I can distinguish individual words
in the buzz of background conversation,
after which it happens a lot,

people stop me on the concourse to ask
if I am who they think I am,
and when I look into their faces,

the slanting, slate gray rain,
some have the eyes of victims,
some, the eyes of torturers.

## AMERICA, AMERICA

The story goes that the day
my grandmother got off the boat,

just a girl from the village,
the dead were parading past

with crumbling, infested faces,
and ever after, she saw,

or, rather, sensed,
the future in her peripheral vision,

God dangling from a broken pulley
and the stars turning black.

## FOR LACK OF A SHOULDER TO CRY ON
The girl in the front seat sobbing
has just failed her road test –

again.

Someone please tell her that the roads
are too crowded anyway,

that there's nowhere worth going
in America you can't get by walking,

that there are worse things
than high school and not having

a best friend, or an ankle bracelet tattoo,
or a driver's license.

Quick, someone please lie.

**THE VICISSITUDES**
Some days I just wake up sad
as if a crow has been at the window

watching me sleep.

Or because the blade of the gravedigger's
shovel rang all night against rock.

Now the landlady blocks the stairs
with large and tragic gestures,

demanding to know is it true
there's a difference, however empty,

between recant and regret.

So many questions, and the only answer
the torn envelope dawn came in.

**BAD NEWS**
Arrives several hours early,
glances frequently at the nameplate

on the door while waiting,
begins to develop a dull headache

from the fluorescents overhead,
the boredom and recirculated air,

but perks up upon recognizing
the provenance of the approaching footsteps

and rehearses one last time what to say,

shoots a large, smoke-blackened tongue
at me as I turn the corner to my office,

and just then the phone in my pocket erupts
and someone somewhere down the hall laughs.

**FALLING**
Hours later, they're still plugging in numbers,

the average annual rainfall in Paris,
the median length of supermarket lines,

working through the night
to calculate the rate of invisible decay,

how many energy drinks must be consumed
for the heart to regain feeling

and for the slow economy to turn around,

the speed at which I fall
from the metal roof into her arms,

the difference in velocity
if I close my eyes or leave them open.

## SINS OF THE FATHER

How can I drink so much
and not be numb

or singing

morose but clear
like the ding

when you drop a coin
into the cigarette vending machine

there's sleep
pouring from my sleeve

instead
and without my consent

just because
I couldn't find the switch

for the lamp
the children either

small and exhausted
making their beds somewhere

under the tangled trees
of the untended orchard

**THE FLOWERS ARE THIRSTY**
I said the pros and cons of a thing
aren't the same as the rights and wrongs,

but you were reading the newspaper,
short paragraphs about the end of the world,

or maybe just pretending,
then again, who am I

to presume to know your heart,
who is anyone,

I'd ask someone else if I could
to unkink the hose,

only, Barbara,

there's no one else here with me
to look into the hot yellow eyes of the daisies.

## AN APOLOGY TO HIS MUSE
Sorry for describing to strangers
the dazzling pink tips of your breasts,

and sorry for the despondent pawnshop
to which I frequently retreat
with another piece of our wedding silver

and for afterward buying the brown pills
that look like .22 longs when I'd said I wouldn't,

and sorry for the police cars howling down
our street as if you were my hostage
and there were a poem, simple but sincere,

pressed like a knife brightly against your throat.

## WESTERN CIV

I call the customer care number

because that's what people
when they have a problem do.

And who is this? the woman
who picks up asks.

Oh, to be a cowpuncher
sleeping it off in the town jail.

## THIS POEM


*for Graham, Jen, Britt & Darla*

I was going to use the names
of the spring flowers in this poem,

but then someone told me,
Forget it, it's already been done,

so I walked down to Starbucks,
where three or more of the nine muses

sometimes hang out,
looking ancient and kind of bored.

Ahoy, bitches, I said,

and they grinned as if they thought
I was in jest.

**LOST JACKET BLUES**
The last time I saw it
it was stepping off

the curb between
parked cars in Cleveland,

its pockets empty
except for

faded receipts
for now-broken items,

its top button loose
and dangling

like the head
of a hanged Nazi,

though others swear
they've since

seen it from behind
secretly scratching

obscene pictograms
and a former phone number

onto glum walls,

notwithstanding which,
I miss it, sometimes.

## SUMMER THUNDER

I plan next summer's garden in my head,
where the bluebells will go,
the sunflowers, with the round faces

and bright yellow haloes
of the martyrs in religious paintings,
all those bloodstained saints

whose lush wounds gleam like wet mouths,
and over here, I'll put pink speedwell,
or maybe purple petunias,

weeping trumpets brokenly announcing
joyful tidings, and over there, the lilies,
licks of orange flame, because what's heaven

without a vestigial concept of hell
and the windows in the house vibrating
to the rumble of ecstatic thunder,

the mammoth heartbeat of God, if God existed.

**HOW IT IS**

The pretty young receptionist
reaches up for a file,

and the tops of her breasts swell
like luminous snow clouds,

and I savor the glimpse,
though a husband and father.

It's just how it is,

the heart hoboes around,
dirty, unshaven, living on handouts.

## SCARECROW

How's it look? I ask,
slipping my arms into the sleeves

of the scarecrow's battered coat.
Good, she says,

but I already know the truth,
and by portentous coincidence,

the sky has just turned the same
disquieting shade of gray

as various diseases of the mind.
I hold my arms out like so

and assume the somber expression,
including opalescent eyes,

of someone remembering something
he wished he didn't,

children overtaken on the road
by claw-footed shadows,

regardless of ancient promises
and the shrill little cries of the sun.

## ALMOST CHRISTMAS

I check my e-mail before going to bed
and find a new message

the Migrant Education Center asking
for a woman's winter coat small or medium

also gloves and a scarf

It's almost Christmas it's getting colder
and she walks her children to school every morning

as people sit at their computers hitting delete

## THE POET CONFRONTS HIS INNER CRITIC

Oh, admit it, it was you
who stole the pencils
from my begging cup,

induced the green parrot
to fly away,
advised me in a dream

to avoid the woods
and the less traveled roads
and keep to the town.

Now you're back,
you bastard, and in winter, too,
my heart crumpling

like red construction paper
when the door suddenly opens,
and just as suddenly closes,

and you call up the stairs
in a voice embedded
with sharp bones of glass

that you're home.

## DESCENT

Our guide smiles shyly at us with neglected teeth.
Every morning we hear of strange new decrees

and arbitrary confiscations. Through the tinted windows
of the tour bus, the sun appears a black disk,

a floating decimal point. We pass veterans who wave
their stumps like tiny flags, women who squat

at the side of the road like dogs to piss, but soon
we'll hardly notice the absence of light or the children

smashing in skulls, scooping out brains, licking their
fingers.

## AT KELLY'S SHAMROCK TAVERN
In the part of town where the porches sag
and evening starts out as an ache,

where the thuggish wind off the dark river
pistol whips the last few pedestrians

and a sweaty woman up in a rented room
moves her broad hips like a jackhammer,

where God has the kind of face he deserves,
the square, brutal forehead of a dirty cop,

I lean on the bar and order a shot and a beer,
and with a cigarette in my fist and the dead

smokestacks of ancient industries to my back,
wait for my luck, or at least the day, to change.

## APOCALYPSE MAMBO

The shadow of the bomber climbs
the Empire State Building

like the red in a thermometer,

and men with French cuffs
decide because they can

whose child drowns in fire,
whose world disappears.

Then they glance at their watches
and gather up their papers,

and we feel dark, insolvent wings
pass over us when least expected,

while shoving it in, or pulling it out,
or reading this.

## THE DYSTOPIAN IMAGINARY

The texts say commit utopia,
take the absent next step,

but the moon-faced babies
drowned in tubs by their mothers

were already there when I got there,
and still there when I left,

wearily wheeling an ash barrel
into the ghostly precincts of dawn,

a stranger's name flowing in loops
of soiled thread just above my heart.

**FOR RECESSIONARY TIMES**
The days pass in shaving my beard
and then growing it back,

but notwithstanding the tall buildings,
it's spring by the calendar

and lewd as the hot, blue tongue
of an acetylene torch.

## THE LOVERS

We're that hole a drunk punched in the sheetrock,
the kind of platitudinous advice everyone gives
but no one ever takes, a couple of misfortune's children
climbing through the squalor of noonday
who eat the wild berries that hang there in the heat
like drops of blood just about to drip.

## THE ELECTRO LUX IMBROGLIO

Whether they throw me down the stairs
or she holds my place in line,

I'll wear something from the Salvation Army
thrift store for the occasion, the crown

of a former prom king, perhaps,
and everyone will laugh at my presumption,

if that is what it is, not least the night watchman,
who, as darkness spreads like a spill,

facetiously swings the feeble yellow beam
of his flashlight this way and that.

## DEAD BEES STING, TOO

It feels more like summer, everyone says,
though only the naturalizing daffodils

have bloomed as I drag the garbage cans
around back, and then you're there,

a peculiar, black-striped pebble of gold plush
that I nudge with the toe of my shoe,

half-suspecting some kind of ruse,

but the rebels in burlap masks have struck,
and the royal escort has fled,

and the gilded coach lies overturned
on a remote road through the dark forest.

## AT THE EDGE OF HISTORY

I am not really here nor
will I be,

but nonetheless

a bum arrives out of
the thin rain

pushing a shopping cart
jammed with abandoned treasures,

old newspapers, broken idols,
the pale, upturned faces of empties,

and when I lie down
in the afternoon,

suffering from an unspecified
heartache,

I can feel through the floor
of all fifty states

the sobbing of an orphan engine.

## SIX WORDS IN SEARCH OF A POEM

They'll be dressed like refugees,
in blankets of yellowing newsprint,

when they limp into view.
You can ask, but they won't tell you

their names, or where they're going,
or why their skin weeps so.

They'll just stare as if remembering
the treachery of the coachman

who abandoned them in a desperate country
while they slept.

Then, after a forlorn conference
with the resident mongrels,

they'll slouch off in the failing light,
accompanied only by heartbroken barking.

## LOVE IS AN ACCIDENT
## WAITING TO HAPPEN

Time is invisible, a patch of black ice,
the other car skidding stately toward us.

What should we do now? What can we?
We're a blur of birthdays and anniversaries

and then gone, catapulted into the ocean of the sky.
Or maybe it's true, there are no such things

as accidents, just questions, whether to love or not
the frenzy of sirens, the emergency road flares,

the volunteer fireman with the red face of a drunk
who impatiently waves his baton in the middle

of the intersection as if conducting an orchestra
only he and the shaken survivors can hear.

**STRANGERS & ANGELS**
A stranger, they say, might be an angel
unrecognizable in the diffuse light

and the enigma of his arrival,

who looks at you as through eyeholes
cut clumsily in a plain paper bag

and relates with ghostwritten words
the events which are about to transpire,

who feels a terrible need to confess
there's a child with your name,

the downcast face of a sunflower
after the birds have scoured it.

# THE GULL

Like a white paper cutout
above the green roof

of the Barnes & Noble
in Poughkeepsie,

it suffers the wind
with the nonchalance

of a soul returning
to the body after sleep

as I cross the parking lot
thinking about something else,

the scab on my heart,
and the traffic on Route 9

waits dejectedly at the light,
a moment like any other

too anonymous to be poetry
and too grievous not to be.

## HOW TO WRITE A STORY

Begin in the middle
with the screams

of something burning,
then insert nightfall

and a trail of bread crumbs
the crows will maliciously eat.

It's important that there be
lost children, but the search dogs

should be tired, or even better,
dubious, and with no way

to stop the bleeding
in the region of the brain

that controls our tears.

## PASTORAL

I stand at the front window
as if I were assigned to stand there

nothing to see

only spring climbing the stairs
with the awkward heaviness

of a pregnant woman

and the tree (apple, I think)
that no longer flowers

lifting its hat in mistaken greeting

## WORDS FOR A FRIEND

So you doubt
that the high school girl
who sulkily took
your order at the drive-
through window
actually wants you
to have a nice day.
Maybe if you told her
how things look
in the emaciated light
of late middle age.
But until then
you might as well try
to smooth out the writing
on the crumpled balls
of paper scattered
about the world.
Or did you expect more
than the consolation
of theoretical happiness?
For Chrissakes, Matt,
don't you know
we're like the junk cars
the fire department
uses to practice rescues?

**SIX PREDICTIONS ABOUT THE FUTURE**

1. There will still be wars, but faraway, happening to other people.

2. Your own experiences will feel like stories someone else made up.

3. Children will disappear into silence, flames, the cellars of monsters.

4. Even the dying will believe in the advertised cures for obscure diseases.

5. Crowds will surge to see gods humiliated and animals hurt.

6. The future will be just like the present – so cold it burns.

## A UNIFIED THEORY OF MOTION

Hard now to distinguish the deranged
from the merely troubled,
or the entrance to all this darkness
from the obsolete exit, so why
even bother when there's the rocking
cradle of her hips, oh, to hell
with everything else, the wreckers
that prowl the charred turnpike,
the breakdowns and chain collisions,
we'll rush each other and sigh
as if our suitcases were packed
and in the hallway and we always
had someplace wonderful to go next.

## TO MEGHAN, ASLEEP IN ETHICS CLASS

As if what people are is all they'll ever be
you close your eyes
and it's suddenly night everywhere and always

nothing can reach you not even

the agitated ghosts of ancient philosophers
swirling around our hot basement classroom
but to you it's just words love death etc.

so why wake you to see the firelight

beating frantically on the walls of Plato's cave
when your sleeping face is beautifully composed
like that of a fairy-tale princess

with a piece of poisoned apple caught in her throat

**TRISTESSE**
It's like being born with a clubfoot
to a family of tightrope walkers

standing there amid the heat and horse droppings
and tornadoes of flies is it still home

even if our parents have vanished
our friends too riding the blacked-out train

beneath the drizzly streets of eternity
everything everyone says sounds

just like something someone said before
and when I look back I can see us in the distance

crashing heads shouting racing our shadows

**A SORT OF SONG**
Where the headstones
wait for our names

under marigold clouds

as leaky as pockets
turned inside out

what is what isn't
requires more

discernment than
compasses possess

but just because
we can't see them

pulsing

like the ragged red campfires
of cowboy angels

doesn't mean love
the stars aren't there

## BURNOUT

I can picture it in my head –
the country of fire,
with a despondent sky,
dead trees like burnt matchsticks.

I've never actually been there,
but I remember the stories men told,
their eyes a brilliant black,
as if they'd just seen falling angels.

Later, when the siren starts up,
I stop on the stairs to listen,
my face characteristically grave,
as if a mask for some archaic ritual.

## WHAT CHARACTERS DO
## WHEN WE'RE AWAY

Lament the heaviness of hard covers,
envy those in the next chapter,
collect adverbs like superstitions,
toss a mini-football back and forth
on the white beach of the margin,
avoid looking at the page number,
know, if only for an instant
when recalling the cold breath
of hands on their skin, how it will end.

**HEARTLAND**
That night in the motel I listened
to the sounds of the highway
and the ragged, decrepit rain,
looking in the only mirror,
the face of a stranger staring back,
taut and slightly tarnished,
like the knuckles of a fist,
and thought about the miles,
how far I'd get tomorrow,
to you, maybe, in Grass Lake,
the heartland, but the next morning
when I started out, it was still dark,
and the maps in the glove box
were old and of the wrong places.

## THE ROOFERS
### *for Gabriel*

It isn't the meaning
of these words

that matters
just the sound

like the hammering
from next door

a couple of roofers
on their knees

and racing the light
because it may be true

what they heard
tomorrow rain

**LOOPS**
I had trouble learning
to tie my shoes,

so my mother took me
to a rabbi. I was five,

maybe six. He demonstrated
on his own shoes first.

Sometimes I think
I dreamed the rabbi

with his long, scary beard.
My mother is dead now.

I still make two loops
and slip one through the other.

## SCHOOLYARD BLUES

They were shouting, Kill him, kill him.
My shirt was torn,

I could feel my eye swelling.
Then he charged,

and I flung my fist out,
and the stone in the ring

I'd just gotten for my 13<sup>th</sup> birthday
sliced open his bottom lip,

an ecstatic gush of blood,
and the fight was over.

We used to call them hoods,
taps on the heels of their shitkickers,

hair Brylcreemed into whorls and curlicues,
but, really, all of us were the same,

beautiful and raw
and pointed like guns toward the future.

**CUSTOMS**
The man in green looks at me narrowly
as if for an explanation of my name, my age,
the half-moons of sweat under my arms.
He asks insidious questions – where, how long,
why – to which I give approximate answers
while my suitcase lies open on the counter
and he bends over the common articles inside
like a doctor delving into a chest wound
to squeeze the small pink ball of my heart.
The line behind me grows numerous,
unaware, or perhaps just unconcerned,
that outside the modern glass terminal,
starving dogs prowl the city in packs
and the smoke of burning tires persists.
The man in green straightens up, nods.
This is whatever sign you say it is,
whatever year of whatever war.

## AT THE NEW ENGLAND
## HOLOCAUST MUSEUM

Puritan-gray evening in Boston,
I find on a long traffic island
suggestions of smokestacks,
the dead rising around me
as serial numbers and exhaust.
Tourists prefer someplace else,
that nameless intersection
familiar from dreams.
But I was always already here,
among the young orphans with old faces
safe under Plexiglas.

## EVENING, COPP'S HILL CEMETERY

Once, before there were children,
we walked among old gravestones
(stained, tilted, corroded teeth)
from which the names had faded,
never thinking we'd be back
and women would still be leaning
gloomy elbows on window sills,
waiting for night to dreamily float
into view, vaporous and immense,
a melting ashen swan.

**DEATH OF THE FROG PRINCE**
Forgive me, frog, for what we did
long ago with our jackknives
behind bunk 6 at Camp Kahagan,
so little blood when we stabbed out
your eyes and laughed at your predicament,
11-year-old boys from all over,
wiping our blades clean on the grass.

**IN EXCELSIS GLORIA**
my daughter thirteen comes home
from school her dark eyes darker
than usual as if her irises had crystallized
because the chorus has been practicing
singing that song in excelsis gloria
for the winter concert she says no way
can she it weirds her out to call jesus
lord savior the singing teacher
when she told him shook his head
deal with it he said and there it is
like the dead bird xylophone our cat
leaves by the front door as a gift
oddly without a mark of violence
on it or any blood just small enough
to fit into my pocket and carry away
if i wish a soft weight a terrible reminder
a secret love note scribbled in haste

# Part 2

# A TINY FUGUE FOR TOMORROWLAND

## EXTRACTS FROM A REVOLUTION

The queen swallows poison from the silver thimble around her neck, but the king trusts that the stroke of the executioner's ax will be clean and true. Reports of miracles reach the capital from throughout the kingdom: love suicides returned to life, God's voice turned to baby's babble. Exhausted celebrants, stinking of drink, sleep in the streets. Now the secret police know who the insomniacs are, and the insomniacs themselves just how interminable the night is.

**WITNESS BOX**

At birth we're given a name we wouldn't choose. Later our parents die to make room for the future. There are regular trains into the city, but few trains out, and the clocks on public buildings are often missing or else wrong. The weather never improves. Some days a hesitant crowd of mothers in black collects outside the former opera house on the basis of a rumor. Oh, how strange to wait to be examined and not know to what extent the testimony will change in the course of transcription.

## NOTES TOWARD AN INVESTIGATION

Although he seems to already know the answer, the investigator asks how the object up there can be the moon when it's spinning like a Ferris wheel. I shrug. He has short, fat fingers like the stumps of melted candles. He asks again would I lend a pyromaniac a light. I concentrate on ignoring the screams coming through the wall. Somewhere I learned the heart is the size of a fist.

## PRESENTIMENT

Last name first middle initial date of birth permanent address mailing address same as above single married education ever convicted if yes explain…It seems I've been applying my whole life for things I don't get. Today I finish quickly, but can't leave, not until the warning sirens stop blaring. The woman at the back counter who takes my application looks like the bitter widow of a paid snitch – something about the doggy wetness of her eyes. I turn away before I realize, or she suspects, that that's what I'm thinking.

## LULLABY FOR THE NAMELESS

The neighborhood children watch with almost scholarly interest the apparatus being dismantled for reassembly downriver. If passing by at such moments, it's best to wear the obedient face my grandfather conspicuously wore throughout his weeks of interrogation. Just think about something ordinary, not these new conscripts cursing and straining as they wrestle the heavy blade onto a lumber wagon, but, for example, the lighted shop windows in the Victorian gloom of evening, or the firing squad back at the barracks listening to the ball game on the radio.

## THE PARABLE OF SUNLIGHT

It's a rare sunny day, but the streets are strangely empty, as if arrests are about to be made, or already have been. Head down, heart revving, I start across the square. The fountain is dry, stained with dead leaves. An old man, with the drab, diligent face of a lifelong student of numbers, scatters bread crumbs for the pigeons. I pretend not to notice – it's safer – and in seconds, reach the far side, where bodies in the early stages of decay hang like gray rags from the trees. I glance back at the old man. He's watching me, and I wonder why and whether tomorrow is supposed to be just as nice as today.

## AT THE MISSING SOLDIERS' OFFICE

The general sits before an open ledger, rubbing his forehead as he studies with mounting perplexity the emerging marks and stains. Although not at fault, the clerks whisper nervously in the background. No matter how many names they erase, or how thoroughly, the ledgers always fill up again by morning. Outside the windows the public hurries past on other errands. These days only dignitaries get to visit the basement museum, where most discover an interest in battle flags, officers' dress swords, and, of course, the shoe full of bones.

## HOMEFRONT

Better stay on your meds. Or get some. Otherwise how will you ignore the pile of hacked-off limbs on the hospital lawn, the amputees limping or crawling away, as disability permits, their sacrifice worse than forgotten – misremembered? You'll end up scribbling on napkins and the last remaining walls, and the scribbles, presuming they're discovered, will sound when pieced together like a suicide note left to mislead investigators. Christ, you'll end up like me, driving slowly over a bridge of bones, your face gray with exhaustion, while along the slatternly, post-industrial river, morning birds sing in the cadaverous trees.

## LATE INNINGS

The man at the ticket window asks for some identification. My dark laughter?  The socket of my missing tooth? I pass through the ancient turnstile. The war is here and it's not, like a book on the nightstand that you'll never open. I'm inconspicuous at the ballpark in my threadbare mourning clothes. The crowd is huge but sullen, as if they know something the players down on the field don't – that the starting pitcher will be betrayed in the late innings by the bullpen, that grass crumbles, that everything that isn't dying is already dead.

**EVACUATION INSTRUCTIONS**
Listen for directions from authorized personnel: which hopeless thoughts to avoid, how long to wait for the destroying angels to tire and the broken buildings to stop burning. Remain inside the train if possible, but if not, open the side door and go out, and love the truculent witnesses to ambiguous events, love witches' gloves, dead men's bells, bloody fingers, love the street dogs that bark dismally and the sunsets that can be beautiful if the light catches the brick dust and swirling ash just so.

## LET IT BURN

Tomorrow is even farther away than we thought, the mottled greenish purple of an old bruise. It doesn't help to shut my eyes. I can still hear gas hissing from shower heads, still feel the sun like a scabrous hand on my back. I promised myself a day-off today, but the ceiling cameras will remember whether I just remained standing here or moved. And what if it's true that the old songs of vanished birds are released when wood from the trees in which they sang is burned? Friends, gather all the fallen branches for a fire.

# Part 3

# GHOSTS OF BREATH

## THE DAUGHTERS OF MAN

I'm high up on a ladder that's noisily being circled by ravens and crows. Somewhere below, my daughters have exchanged names. I call to the younger one, but the older one answers. I should've known this is what happens when you marry late. They laugh at my confusion and then head off through the trees. It isn't that they don't love me; it's just that they love other things more. I begin to climb down. I'm halfway to the ground before I ever notice the man in the skeleton mask pacing at the bottom.

## THE HEART BREAKS DOWN
## LIKE A MECHANICAL DEVICE

The repairman says mice have chewed through the wires. Thank you, I say – to the mice. Maybe now I can think without being interrupted. But first I must do something about the Styrofoam peanuts scattered all over the floor, and then there's the fire to strum and the Bureau of Weights and Measures to contact. My wife won't be any help. She's hiding in our bedroom, embarrassed that we have grown children. I pat my pockets as if searching for cigarettes, or, if not cigarettes, symptoms. One side of me is cold and dark; the other side, cold and bright. I exchange melancholy glances with the deer head on the wall. The repairman says he'll be right back. Quiet, I say, the baby's sleeping.

## DOG YEARS

The war has entered its second decade. Maddened by the futility, the dogs run away. Few people seem to notice that they're gone. Three times a day, if not more, their former owners take empty leashes out for a walk. Just this morning the old widow stopped to let a boy on his way to school bend down and scratch behind the ears of what wasn't there.

## GHOSTS OF BREATH

I was sitting on the curb, resting, when my father called. "We've lost your mother," he moaned. Where could she be? I got back on my bike and rode down to the pond. The swans hadn't seen her. Neither had the winos sleeping under the bushes. A plane passed high overhead as if on a bombing run. I got out of my car. It was a neighborhood of mud streets and old stone houses. I stood gazing through a window, marveling at the changing colors of the flames. The town constable caught me. "Move on!" he barked. He raised his club threateningly. And now I'll never know whether the woman who lived there with her shadow had just left or was about to return.

## ALMOST NIGHT

I step down off the bus and back into the world. The landscape smells as if it has just been painted. Red fields stretch away on either side. I can't imagine what's growing. By the time I hurry into the village, I'm frightened. Everyone I'd passed on the road, man or woman, had the thick, unfinished features of a convict. I find a door in the wall, a place for a drink. There's only one other patron. He might be a slaughtering angel. He looks at me over the rim of his glass as if he were, and I know then that, despite the time, it's almost night.

## INVESTIGATIONS INTO THE TECTONICS OF THE TIBETAN PLATEAU

The chief inspector leans back in his chair and picks his teeth with a matchstick. The dead aren't missing much, he muses. My right arm hangs dead at my side. Perhaps I'm bleeding from somewhere as well. His men, spread out across the plateau, rap smartly on the doors of empty apartments. I only escape because they let me. But the moon is chipped, and even the star-strung ladder on which I might once have climbed wobbly toward it is gone.

## FUGITIVE PIECES

Come morning, I'll renew my flight, a hat and scarf to hide my face and a pill sewn in the lining of my pocket in case of capture. I'll pass through small towns God has abandoned, where the stoplights work, but traffic is frozen. I'll hear guerrilla fighters scurrying about the tunnels beneath the soybean fields. I'll sleep less and less and sigh more and more. I'll be hungry all the time. As in a legend, the ravens will feed me.

# Part 4

# ABANDONED BUT STILL BURNING

**TRUE ROMANCE**
We discuss in whispers how to do it,
standing up or lying down or front to back,

but by the time we decide,
the workers have returned from break

and are attacking the building
with sledgehammers and crowbars.

Maybe tomorrow, she says, getting out of bed.

## ARIA FOR MY DAUGHTER

She hears the slow thunder of a piano.
She wonders where exactly she is –
a new suburb of disappointment, perhaps.
She follows the red thread of the wind
as it twists inland.
She passes a huddle of secretaries
on their smoking break.
She can describe if they ask
the feeling of floating above thunder
on her belly and then her back.
She sees out the corner of her eye buildings
dissolving into particles and waves.
She tilts her face as for a kiss.
She sings in Italian though she's never spoken it.

## WINTER SOLDIERS

Can't you feel it,

the troops dimly massing
on the border,

horses the color of doom
dragging cannons

along old lumber roads,
their hooves muffled with cloth,

as the collaborators among us
count down the days

till monotonous petals of snow
will be falling murderously

everywhere.

**AMONG THE DEAD**
They don't ask for a lot,

a pound of nails
to hold the lid in place,

a story to help them
fall back asleep,

and now and then
the loan of a handkerchief,

which they always return,
when they remember to return it,

crumpled and stained.

**RIGHT-HAND MAN**
I'd pick up a spoon
in my left hand,

and they'd take it
and put it in my right.

I was small, very small,
probably no bigger

than a hobo's bindle.
They'd look down at me

while I slept
and shake their heads.

Where they came from,
liars and arsonists

were left-handed.
I'd pick up a block

in my left hand,
and they'd take it

and put it in my right.
Now sometimes

when I start to reach
for what I want,

I'll stop suddenly
and wonder

whose hand this is.

## AUTUMN SONATA

When the tree, in high dudgeon, suddenly
pushes through the polished wood floor,

and the congregation of small scared birds
disbands in confusion,

when the deaf despise the hearing,
and the night janitor at the Museum of Mad Ideas

wipes with special care
the shatterproof glass under which

Hitler's voice rages,
time's up,

and I shed my coat on the ground
and lie down beside her,

believing,
as we curl gratefully into each other,

what is real is whatever is
faded or broken or falling.

# A MATTER OF PREFERENCE
Wouldn't you rather
we walk down

the avenues of rain
trading verses from Poe

like black roses
and only take

our best memories
with us and the small

butterfly tattoo
on the back of your neck

wouldn't you rather
the government

forgot our faces
our names and when

we're faraway
and finally beyond

the boom of waves
wouldn't you rather

I put my hand
in the flame

between your legs
well I would

## REVISIONIST HISTORY

When she asks what I did all day
while she was gone,

what should I say, that I cut
four lines from a poem

I wrote last week and then later,
on second thought, put them back?

Probably not.

Better to shrug or be curt, almost defiant,
like the red door of a white church.

**LATE SLEEPER**
You who stayed up too late last night,
get up, get up, everyone else is already up.

The world is an incomplete sentence
without you. I know the leaves are yellowing,

and it's cold, but get up, please, get up,
and look out the back window. There are

emergencies, clouds, acts of contrition,
light-up letters as big as small children,

sometimes even bigger.

## PUMP AND LADDER

My grandfather had a bad heart.
The doctors warned him

about smoking a pack a day
and drinking slivovitz,

the plum brandy that tastes
like nail polish remover smells,

but he didn't listen.

One day he collapsed in the street.
Someone screamed.

Someone else ran to the firehouse for help.
A fireman who had been shining

a fire truck, a pump and ladder, ran out.
My grandfather looked dead.

He wasn't moving at all.
He wasn't even moaning.

The fireman gave him mouth-to-mouth.
People later said it was lucky

he collapsed right outside a firehouse.
Otherwise, they said, he wouldn't be here.

Then my grandmother got sick and died,
and my parents got old themselves.

They put my grandfather into a nursing home.
He would quietly unzip and pee in the hall.

## EVERYTHING SIMPLE
## BECOMES COMPLEX

The phones are dead, our children, unreachable,
unless that's one of them crying in the street.

Everything simple has become complex.
I should've known we'd be abandoned

to vandals and the weather,
and, before heartbreak had vaporized,

admitted to the priesthood of grief,
but my thoughts were taken up with other things,

the advantages of probity versus confession.
Now the three-legged black dog next door,

moved by the poor moon's blistered face,
growls all night in grisly sympathy.

## ELEGY FOR THE NEWBORN

The librarian doesn't care
as she once might have
that the books I'm returning
are missing some words.
Then I come to a forest,
dark, mossy clouds
like morbid thoughts
not even drugs can dispel.
A yellow cab, its engine running,
is always waiting at the curb
for a messiah to appear.
It's the difference between
a democracy and a republic,
and though there's no wind,
the puddles shiver.
My face reminds most people
of someone they knew long ago,
before the assassinations
and roadside bombings.
I stop to rest with the newborn
on the border of shrill gulls.

## VARIATIONS ON AN ENIGMA

Great mathematicians peering down
from the roof might be able

to compute in their heads
how many steps it'd take me

to cross the street while bleeding,
and if they cared and weren't

constantly being accosted
by counterfeit pleas from near hysterics,

they'd be as surprised as I am
that my beard is coming in gray

and add a few more zeroes,
for I was told – no, assured –

the sutures would dissolve,
the heart eventually grow back,

only to arrive early this morning
to an unwashed blackboard,

empty desks,
a note blown on the floor,

the ink still damp.

**DOG STAR MAN**
Innocent or not, the arrestees
enter the court building

in cuffs and with downcast eyes.
All science, Bronowski said, is a search

for unity among hidden likenesses.
Might as well stay on the line

for the next available operator.
You can hear if you really listen

the common names for things
weeping noisily beneath the music.

# NOTES ON EMPATHY

**1**

This isn't silence, but forgery,
the thick rubber soles
of the nighttime attendant.

**2**

Who are we?
Only the very people we seek,
the ones who abandoned
their cars in the road
with the doors flung open.

**3**

It rained on my birthday,
but what do you care,

it wasn't your birthday,
and it isn't raining still.

And besides,
you have a new haircut.

**ARMY NAVY**
Just as the dog-headed priests long ago foretold,
there's a former Army Navy store

with boarded-up windows when I step outside
and Department of Social Services recipients

resigned to waiting on the bench for a bus
that's half a lifetime late and may never arrive.

So tell me again why, despite gravity,
I shouldn't gradually disappear for a while

like the broken eggshell of moon
and come back in the spring as someone else,

wry, salacious, *au fait*, with a straw-colored beard
and an increasing love for real things –

the smell of institutional floor wax, for example,
or a souvenir shot glass from Hershey Park

that fits my dank hand, which now, coincidentally,
lies against an imperturbable machine

whose mechanisms are both ingenious and precise,
but whose purpose is, like sadness, amorphous.

## LOOKING FOR WORK, WEEK 5

"You aren't quite right for us," he says.

He isn't looking at me when he says it.
He's looking at the screen of his cell phone.

Where to now?
It's a hot day, and it promises to get hotter.

I start walking.
The folder tucked under my arm
might as well be empty for all the good
the papers inside have done me.

A woman up ahead
has a lovely, heart-shaped ass.

I can feel the sweat break out on my back.
I'm not sure this is the right direction.
My legs ache.
There's a metallic taste in my mouth

I tell myself this is the right direction.
I breathe in, I breathe out.

Etc. and so on.

## BLACK FRIDAY

The shopkeepers of New Hope, PA,
will open their doors at midnight tonight,

though shelves are collapsing
and shoppers will be scant,

just a couple fat women as indistinguishable
from each other as houseflies

who'll enter gasping for breath
because of the steep climb

and gaze around at the debris,
used condoms and old candy wrappers

and chunks of plaster, before asking
the only salesgirl on the floor not crying

whether the fire pictured in the circular
comes in another color besides this red.

## MY FATHER, KAFKA

Here's an old photo of my father
oddly alone on a city street,
he's as slim as a novella
and dark as a gypsy prince,
he looks like Kafka,
thick, black hair slicked back
and comet-bright eyes,
the wariness of someone
suddenly summoned to appear
at such and such a time
at such and such a place,
the Workers' Accident Insurance Institute
for the Kingdom of Bohemia,
and he's on his way there now,
hands thrust deep in his pockets
as if to hide certain injuries,
but, of course, this is not K.,
and that is not Prague behind him,
and I am not born.

## A DREAM

The chair was tilted back. My mouth was open.
He reached in with a pair of pliers.
They were the pliers from my household toolbox.
I became aware of music, something classical,
playing discreetly in the background
The tooth was stubborn. He grunted as he yanked at it.
I wondered why I was there, what I had done.
In the outer office, voices were arguing.
He yanked harder. Sweat dripped down his face.
I looked at the brown stains on the ceiling
to avoid looking further at him.
We stayed like that for hours, perhaps days.
It got so bad that even the birds,
with their wild, tiny hearts, flew away.

## COLD ENOUGH TO SNOW

That's me, the one staring straight ahead
as if maybe if I stared long enough
the things passing in front of me would change,
the panhandler with the unfortunate stains
on his pants would find a twenty or the dead flowers
in the trash would come back to life, but it's cold
on the corner and getting colder every morning,
and I'm waiting, tired of waiting, still waiting
for the yellow school bus of the sun to pick us up.

## FIELD TRIP

The big, dirty white tent squats
in the mall parking lot

like a derelict god taking a dump.
How pale the inmates look

from their long confinement
and how confused they look, too,

to be allowed out on a field trip.
None remember why they were put away,

this one for tampering with odometers,
that one for throwing folding chairs

around the church rec room,
and now they can't remember why

they're here either, whether as reward
for good behavior or as further punishment.

The chaperons, dressed in orange safety vests,
refuse to say, but only smile and nod

and point toward the dark and narrow opening,
just inside which darker shapes shimmer.

It's noon, or a little later, and as the inmates wait
in line with all the others on the hot blacktop,

they can already feel their skin beginning to burn.

## ABANDONED BUT STILL BURNING
What's with the defeatist attitude?
So you found a torn-off wing

stuck under your windshield wiper.
How many birds do you think

visit major American cities each year?
At least you weren't beaten

by the drunks in the bleachers
for wearing your funeral suit.

Then you would've hardly heard
the singing or seen the line of refugees

from the famine. I'm telling you,
Relax. The candlelight we're carrying

between us like a sheet of glass
is the very light we need.

And if the German wolf pack
happens to return to prowl

the sea lanes, we can always wave
goodbye to them with the other hand.

# THE INVISIBLE WAR

**1**
The sirens startle us.
We sit up in bed,

only to lie back down.
Our faces are

next to each other,
close enough for a kiss.

Instead, we exchange
medieval looks

of fear and doubt.


**2**
As we walk past Sal's Place
holding hands,

the daytime drinkers
in the window

look away,
embarrassed.

Unless it isn't us
they're considering,

but the story of gunships
clattering over rooftops,

an infant later found
crawling in the rubble
in the elaborate harness
of a seeing-eye dog.

**FATHERLY ADVICE**

Wear hunter's camouflage.
You don't want to be
one of those people,
do you, whose goal in life
is simply to stand there
and look good?
Your grandmother was,
and the soldiers tore
a crying baby from her arms
and flung it on the fire.
Therefore, every day,
practice invisibility.
Plunge through intersections –
the busier, the better –
just as the light turns red.
Move often and without regret,
and leave no obvious trail,
no broken twigs and such, to follow.
The devil is upstairs humping
a pillow, pretending that it's you.

# Part 5

# SLEEP RITUALS

## SUBMISSION GUIDELINES

Send us the pain you squeezed from your first child's
first hurt but avoid gratuitous references to atom
smashers we prefer the historical Jesus spare parts for
fire trucks a story translated into battered English about
growing up in a double wide tell us you rinse with beer
before bed even if it isn't true include boat people in
tuxedo shirts waiting tables clouds building off the coast
your Times Roman face the one you use when you look
out the window where it's always raining

## SLEEP RITUALS

Tonight, like most nights, she goes to bed first, and he stays up to test the machine, standing where the light is good and no one can see him from the street. He pops off the lid using gentle thumb pressure. Inside, heating coils glow like the ribs of a starving dog, God rolls dice that have no spots, a mare with a burning mane screams in terror. He bends at the waist for a closer look. After a moment's argument with himself, he plunges his hand into the smoke. It feels cold, and a spider-web of scaffolding begins to rise around the dark castle of a line of mad kings. He weeps as if it were his own heart he was dismantling. Soon he'll be tired enough to sleep, and when she awakes before the alarm, the dawn will be full of birdsong and the birdsong, as sometimes happens, full of primitive grief.

**FIRST LIGHT**

Running I tripped on the uneven pavement broke my two front teeth it wasn't my fault I was crying and bleeding when my father got home from the factory and saw my ruined mouth he walloped me across the face whaddaya stupid he said my mother couldn't hit hard arthritis so she beat me with a hairbrush for wasting paper which is what she called my drawing I don't think about it often or the birds in the window box with black skullcaps like observant Jews their cheeping would wake me as if first light had become suddenly audible until my mother noticed them there and told my father who cursing opened my bedroom window that Sunday and reached out a dark and sparkling hand and destroyed as I watched in pale silence the circle of their nest

## AT THE SIGN OF THE MORTAR & PESTLE

Who'll turn the witch's broom back into a tree? Who'll make the sick baby to crawl again? You? Ha! Somehow I don't think so. But step inside the shop. An odd but not unpleasant odor. Cellophane packets of ground bone arrayed on the counter. Shelves lined with well-stoppered bottles. A Mason jar in which an unidentifiable pink organ floats. Necklaces of wildflowers hanging from hooks. And over there in the far corner, his pale eyes narrowed in concentration, the apothecary's assistant breaking long, stiff strands of hair, rather like your own, into a furiously boiling pot.

## THE PEDAGOGY OF THE POSSESSED

The teacher stands swaying at the front of the classroom. Many of the students think he must be drunk. His face is flushed, and his hands flutter like disoriented birds as he speaks in desperate tones about black holes, carnivores, ancient Babylon. But he isn't drunk; he's merely over-prepared. In the faculty lounge the older teachers laugh at his earnestness. They feel superior because he hasn't realized yet that when he turns to write something on the board, the students vanish – true, some only momentarily, but others forever.

## THE DEATH OF THE BOOK

They were standing on the lawn and the driveway. He thought he saw some sneaking around the side of the house. They were chanting something. He hesitated to ask his wife what it was. It sounded like "Kill, kill, kill the book." And were those staves they were waving? They looked like staves. Where the hell did they get staves? Not at the Home Depot. He couldn't understand their level of outrage. Their faces were distorted by a vicious mixture of anger, hate, fear, and disgust. All he had done was write a book. OK, so it wasn't the greatest book ever written. It wasn't *The Red and the Black* (which, come to think of it, wasn't the greatest book ever written either). But it was the best he could do at the time. He had alligator-wrestled thousands of words into submission. He had sat down to the computer whether he felt inspired that day or not. He had sacrificed his nerves and strained his brain cells. "Why?" he asked as he stared out the window at the growing crowd. "Why?" Although it was clearly a rhetorical question, his wife attempted to answer it. "Because," she said, "life is too short to read a bad book." She brushed a tear from her eye and added, "Especially a long one."

**WHY THE FACE**

Because the road climbs as though attracted by the form of a mountain. Because she has her sleeve rolled up and a snarling dragon tattoo. Because certain lies are best told in legal language. Because the machine accepts only quarters. Because Freud said whether it happens for real or happens in dreams it happens. Because matter echoes like an accidental gunshot. Because the graves are desecrated but the borders guarded. Because it isn't raining. Because later it might.

## GIANT KILLER

The giant flees helter-skelter down the street, noisily pursued by the neighborhood dogs. I can't see a beanstalk anywhere, only some white, scallop-edged clouds pasted on an endless blue sky.

The barking grows fiercer. In his panic and confusion, the giant trips on the uneven cobblestones. Maybe it's the drugs everyone took in college, or the years of road rage since then, but people just step around him, pretending he isn't lying there, huge and helpless.

Later, when school lets out, the children will cautiously approach the spot. They'll hold out their cell phones and take his picture, as if all the porn in the world has metastasized to their hearts.

## BLOOD AND FEATHERS

Hands clasped behind their backs, the doctors of moral philosophy used to wander through the park lost in thought. Now they terrorize the swans with their motorized wheelchairs. The man raking the gravel path does his best to reconcile himself to the blood and feathers. He has even developed a theory concerning the chemical basis of evil. In his room at the boardinghouse he keeps a black-framed wedding picture of his parents to which he talks all night about it. But only the boy in the sailor suit, squinting up at the sun as he waits for a friend, ever supposes that the sky can be folded in squares like a map, taken home, and hidden.

## THE EXTRUDED PLASTIC LITURGY

Something there. I touch the top of my head to find out
what, and my startled fingers come away with blood.
Such signs and wonders abound, even when approaching
the tourists outside a museum of useless and enigmatic
objects for change.

*

I cry at the movies and later that night dream I'm being
led through the distorted faces of the laughing crowd in
cuffs.

*

The wind is still as if it also is contemplating the dark.
Quick, send the extruded plastic moon to this address,
and because the ambulance driver will get lost in the
maze of small, unlighted streets, send the moon out for
an encore.

# LOVE, DEATH, ETC.

**1**

My mother scoops snow off the fire escape into the kitchen pot. Her hands dart like birds. I'm four, maybe five. It's snowing for the first time, but I'm sick with something and can't go out. She carries the snow to the bathtub where she bathes my brother and me, scrubbing us in a kind of rage until our skin is as rosy as the bottoms of angels. After she dumps the snow from the pot, I kneel outside the tub and play with it, not knowing what I'll remember one day or that no one escapes the fire.

**2**

Someone asks, "Have you written anything yet about your mother's death?" No . . . no, I haven't. There aren't any angels to consult, and if there were, they'd hurl themselves like despondent drunks onto the gleaming knives and spears of the spires below. Instead, only birds scatter at the approach of dark, and I try not to see too much, the forgeries and desecrations, or the black snow collecting on the floor of my heart.

**3**

Then it's spring, a year since the failed operation, the road into town smeared with blood and entrails, and a quorum of crows crowding around what's left, hungry, contentious, but to me, simply driving past, it looks different, like a blob of God's spit.

**4**

Where we sleep, you know, it isn't necessarily where we wake up, it all depends on what we dream, my dead mother, for example, crisscrossed by the fence, fingers hooked through the diamond-shaped links.

# ACKNOWLEDGEMENTS

Special thanks to the reviews that previously published select poems from this collection:

2River View, "At the New England Holocaust Museum" and "Evening, Copp's Hill Cemetery"
55 Words, "How to Write a Story" and "What Characters Do When We're Away"
Alba, "The News at 11," "Dead Bees Sting, Too," and "Night Must Fall"
Bartleby Snopes "Extracts From a Revolution," "Witness Box," "Notes Toward an Investigation," "Presentiment," "Lullaby for the Nameless," "The Parable of Sunlight," "At the Missing Soldiers' Office," "Homefront," "Late Innings," "Evacuation Instructions," and "Let It Burn"
Best Poem, "Six Words in Search of a Poem"
Bijou Poetry Review, "The Daughters of Man"
Bolts of Silk, "A Sort of Song"
Centrifugal Eye, "Snapdragon Clawhammer" and "Love During Wartime"
Cerebral Catalyst, "The Gull"
Corduroy Mountain, "Investigations into the Tectonics of the Tibetan Plateau"
Defenestration, "Death of the Book"
Dogzplot, "Apocalypse Mambo," "Six Predictions About the Future," "The Heart Breaks Down Like a Mechanical Device," and "Variations on an Enigma"
Drunk & Lonely Men, "Black Friday"

Elegant Thorn Review, "Strangers & Angels" and
"Loops"
elimae, "The Dystopian Imaginary," "The Electro Lux
Imbroglio," "At the Edge of History," "The Extruded
Plastic Liturgy," "Dog Star Man," and "Notes on
Empathy"
First Thought, "Western Civ," "Song for Recessionary
Times," and "The Lovers"
Flutter Poetry Journal, "The Vicissitudes" and "Autumn
Sonata"
The Foliate Oak, "Scarecrow" and "Burnout"
Getting Something Read, "Late Sleeper"
Gold Wake Press,  "Fugitive Pieces"
Hanging Moss Journal, "At the Sign of the Mortar and
Pestle" and "Pedagogy of the Possessed"
Holy Cuspidor, "This Poem"
JMWW, "Tristesse"
Journal of Heroin Love Songs, "How It Is" and "A
Matter of Preference"
JuiceBox, "Aria for My Daughter"
Kora, "Submission Guidelines" and "Blood and
Feathers"
Mannequin Envy, "Love Is an Accident Waiting to
Happen"
Neon, "Lovesick," "Identity," and "Lost Jacket Blues"
New Verse News, "America, America," "Almost
Christmas," and "Winter Soldiers"
Niteblade, "Giant Killer"
online whispers & [Shouts], "Revisionist History"

Opium, "Pump and Ladder" and "Looking for Work,
Week 5"
The Orange Room Review, "For the Woman Who
Walked Out During My Reading," "For Lack of a
Shoulder to Cry On," "An Apology to His Muse," and
"Cold Enough to Snow"
Plum Ruby Review, "In Excelsis Gloria"
Poetry Flyer, "Unified Theory of Motion"
Poetry Friends, "The Flowers Are Thirsty" and
"Summer Thunder"
Poetry Journal, "Descent"
Prairie Poetry, "Heartland"
Prick of the Spindle, "Sleep Rituals" and "First Light"
qarrtsiluni, "Elegy for the Newborn" and "Everything
Simple Becomes Complex"
Raving Dove, "Schoolyard Blues" and "Dog Years"
Review Americana, "The Poet Confronts His Inner
Critic" and "The Roofers"
Right Hand Pointing, "A Note to Reader," "Two
Laments & a Song," "Ditty," "Haircut," "A Cure for
Boredom," "Bad News," "Falling," and "My Father,
Kafka"
The Rose & Thorn, "Love, Death, Etc."
Shoots & Vines, "Fatherly Advice" and "Field Trip"
Silenced Press, "To Meghan, Asleep in Ethics Class"
Stirring, "Customs"
The Stone Table Review, "Pastoral"
THE, "Sins of the Father" and "A Dream"
tinfoil dresses, "Almost Night"
Wilmington Blues, "Death of the Frog Prince"

Howie Good, a journalism professor at the State University of New York at New Paltz, is the author of eight poetry chapbooks, including *Police and Questions* (2008) from Right Hand Pointing, *Tomorrowland* (2008) from Achilles Chapbooks, *The Torturer's Horse* (2009) from Recycled Karma Press, and *Love Is a UFO* (2009) from Pudding House. He has been nominated three times for a Pushcart Prize and twice for the Best of the Net anthology. *Lovesick* is his first full-length book of poetry.

www.ingramcontent.com/pod-product-compliance
Lightning Source LLC
Chambersburg PA
CBHW031300060726
47590CB00003B/988